How to Draw

For Kids

Author Tony R. Smith

Copyright © 2019 by Tony R. Smith. All Rights Reserved. No part of this publication may be reproduced, distributed, or transmitted in any form or by any means, including photocopying, recording, or other electronic or mechanical methods, or by any information storage and retrieval system without the prior written permission of S.S. Publishing, except in the case of very brief quotations embodied in critical reviews and certain other noncommercial uses permitted by copyright law

Big Face Circle Method

CIRCLES ARE USED TO HELP CREATE YOUR DRAWING.

CIRCLE

Oval Circle Method

OVAL CIRCLES ARE USED TO HELP CREATE YOUR DRAWING IN 8 STEPS.

Plain Circle Method

PLAIN CIRCLES ARE USED TO HELP CREATE YOUR DRAWING.

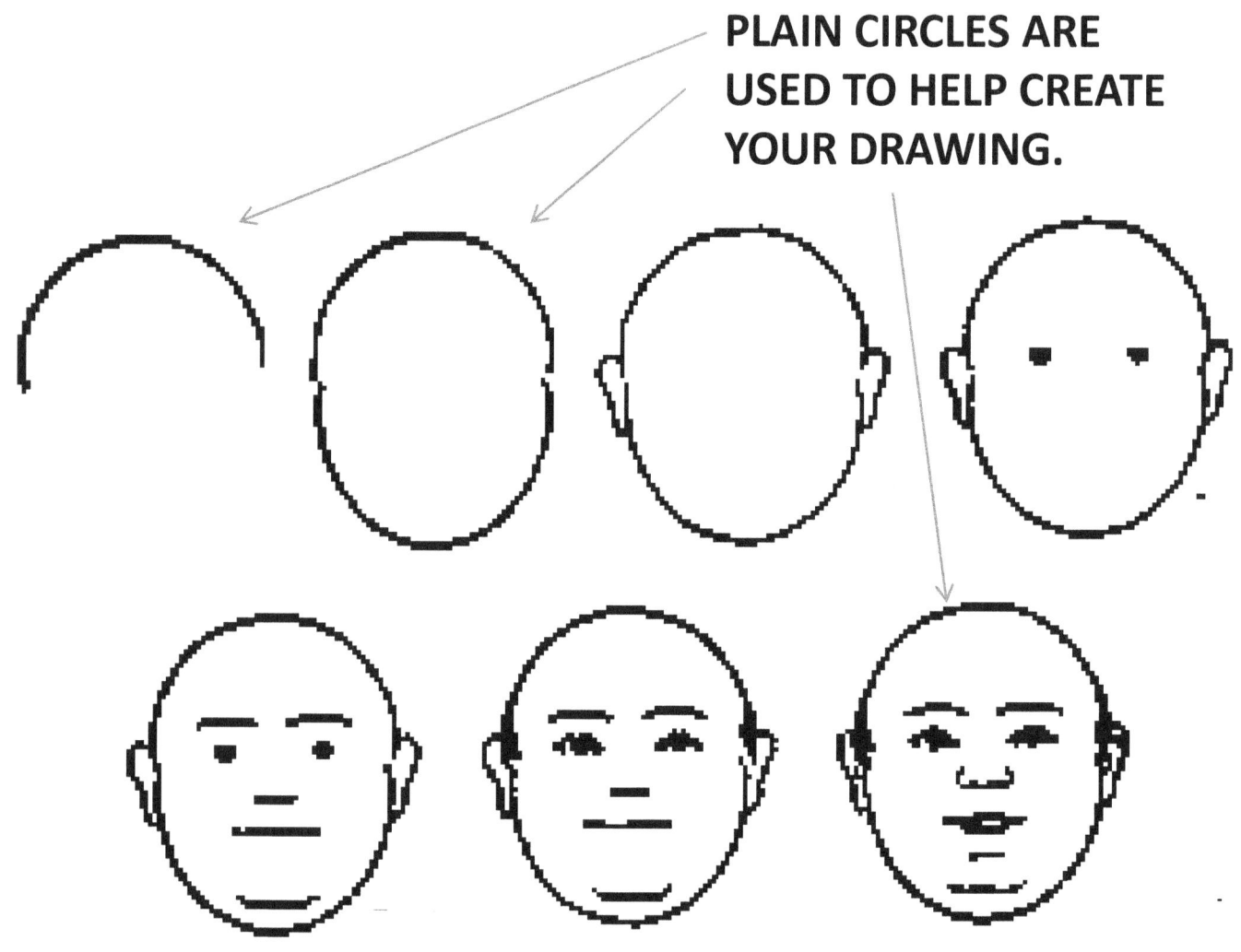

Line Method

LINE METHOD CAN HELP TO CREATE YOUR DRAWING IN 6 STEPS.

Lines and Shade

THE LINES AND SHADE METHOD CAN HELP TO CREATE YOUR DRAWING IN 1 STEP.

Side Drawing Method

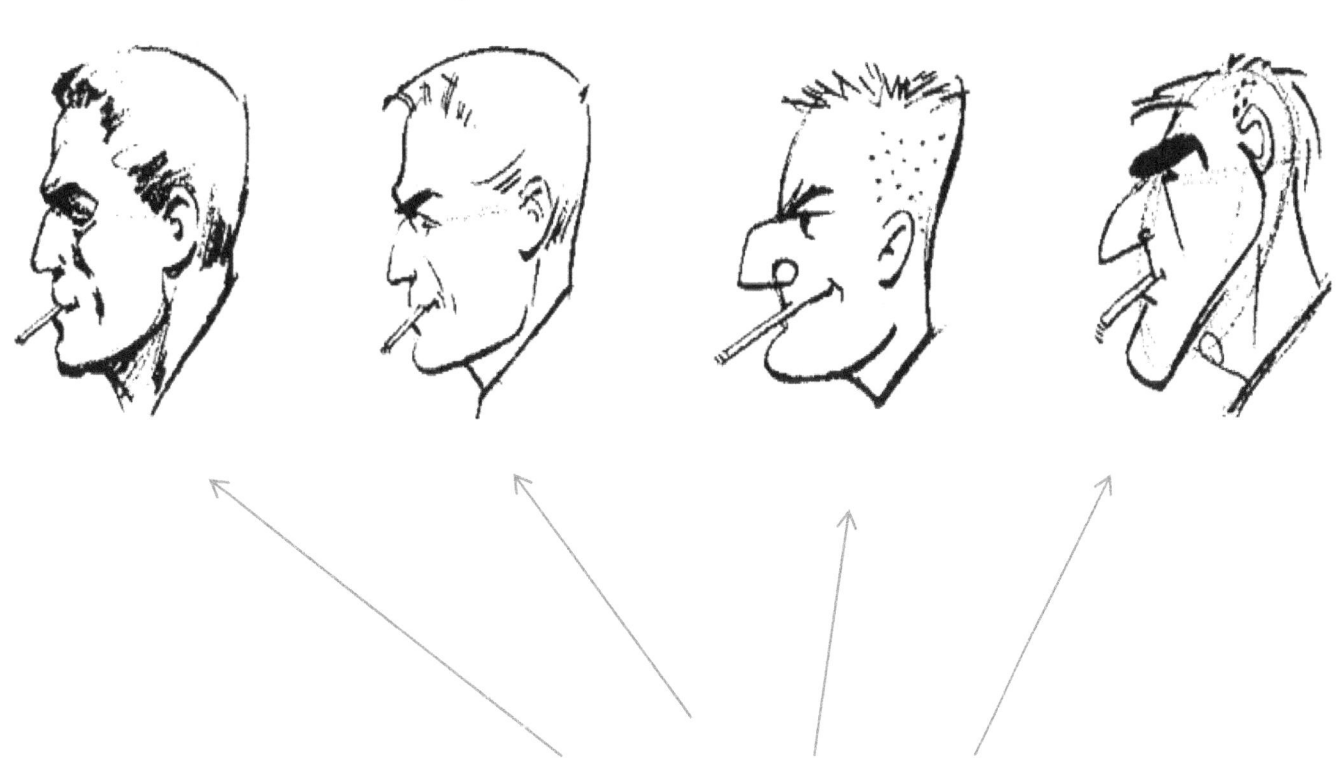

THE SIDE DRAWING METHOD WILL GIVE YOUR DRAWING A DIFFERENT FEEL AND VIEW.

Straight Line Method

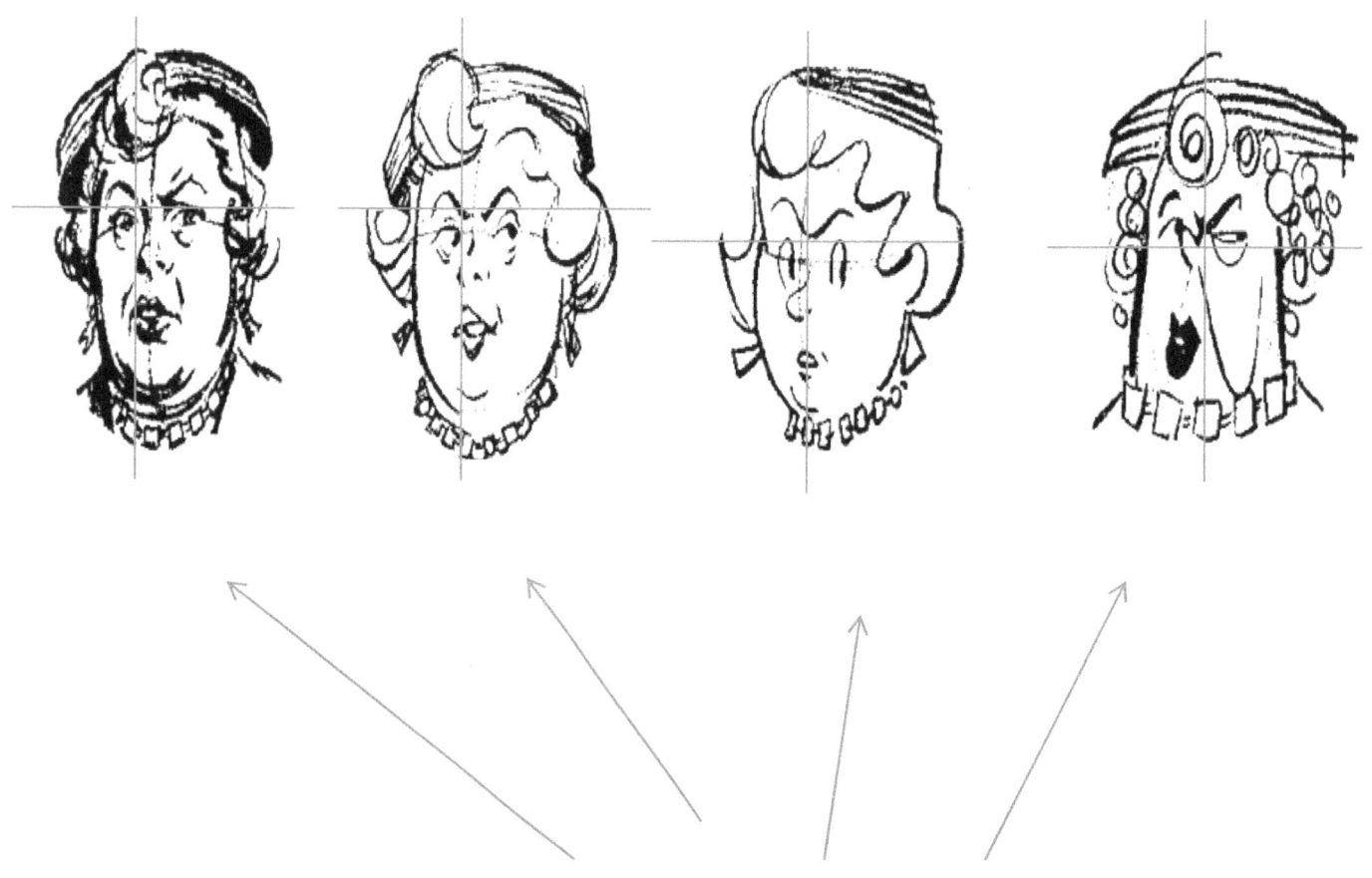

THE STRAIGHT LINE DRAWING METHOD WILL CENTER YOUR DRAWING SO ALL PARTS MATCH UP.

Line Cross Method

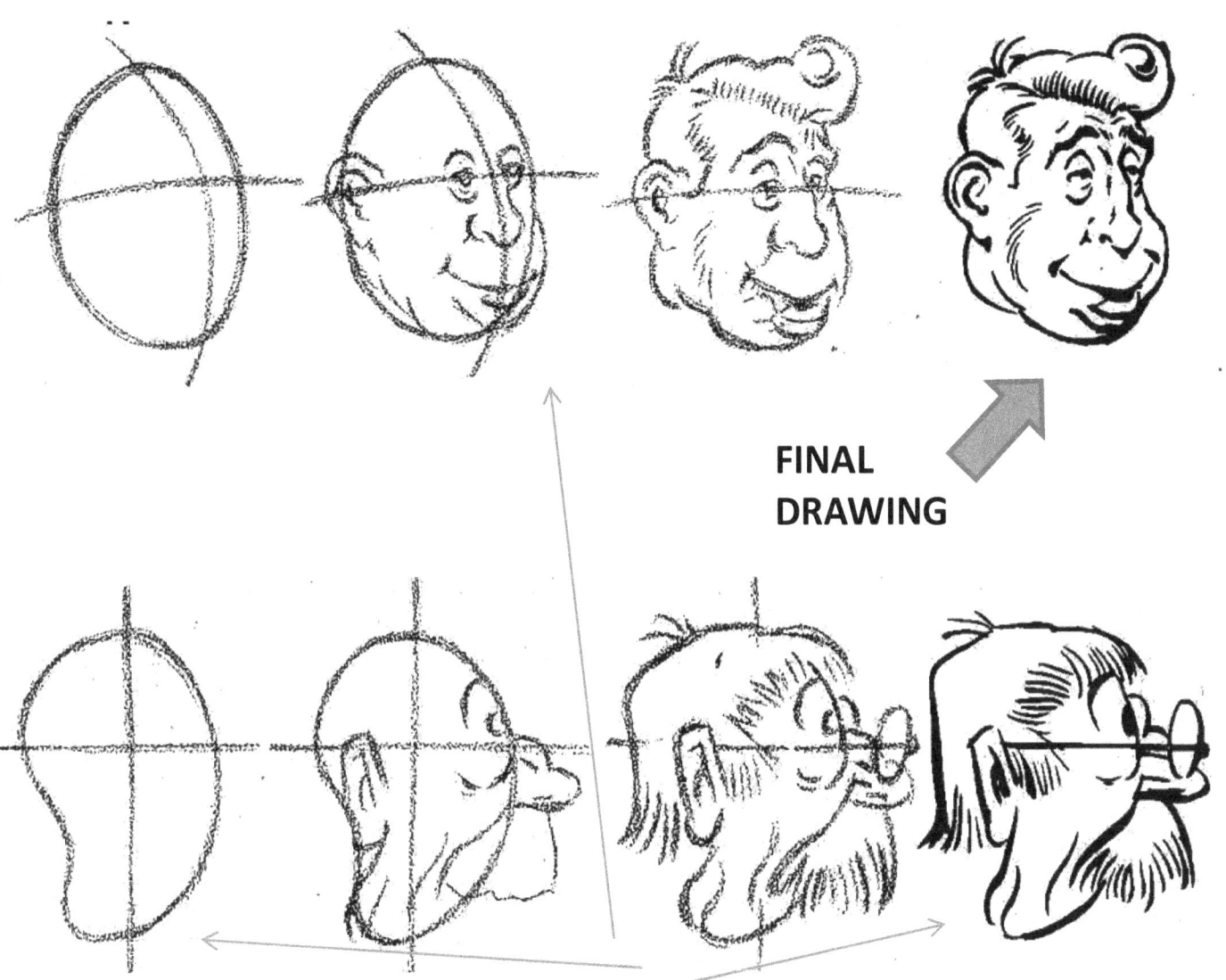

FINAL DRAWING

THE LINE CROSS DRAWING METHOD WILL GIVE YOUR DRAWING A DIFFERENT FEEL AND VIEW/SIDE AND SIMI CIECLE.

Circle Method

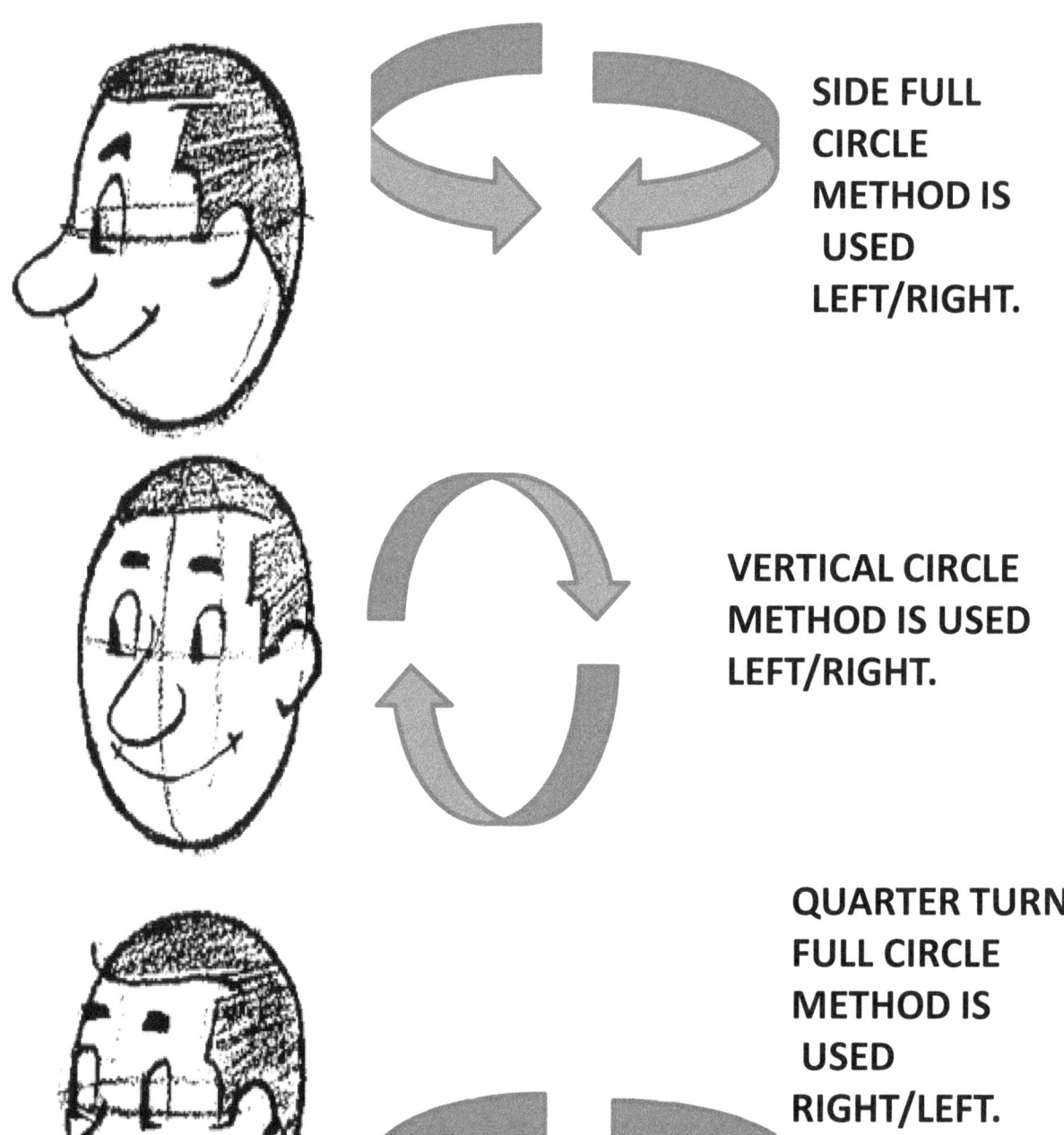

SIDE FULL CIRCLE METHOD IS USED LEFT/RIGHT.

VERTICAL CIRCLE METHOD IS USED LEFT/RIGHT.

QUARTER TURN FULL CIRCLE METHOD IS USED RIGHT/LEFT.

Cylinders and Circles

CYLINDERS AND CIRCLE METHOD CAN BE USED TO CREATE ODD HEAD SHAPES LIKE MONSTERS OR ALIENS.

Face Progression

FACE PROGRESSION CAN BE USED TO AGE THE DRAWING FROM YOUNGER TO OLDER.

Box Drawing

BOX DRAWINGS ARE USED TO CREATE DRAWING WITH SMALL DETAILS FOR A TIGHT FIT.

PLAIN HEAD

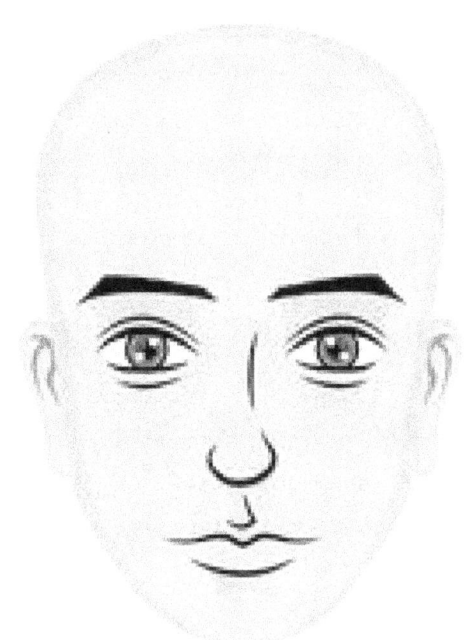

DRAW/SKETCH

TWO HEADS

DRAW/SKETCH

GIRL HEAD

DRAW/SKETCH

BLANK HEAD STYLES

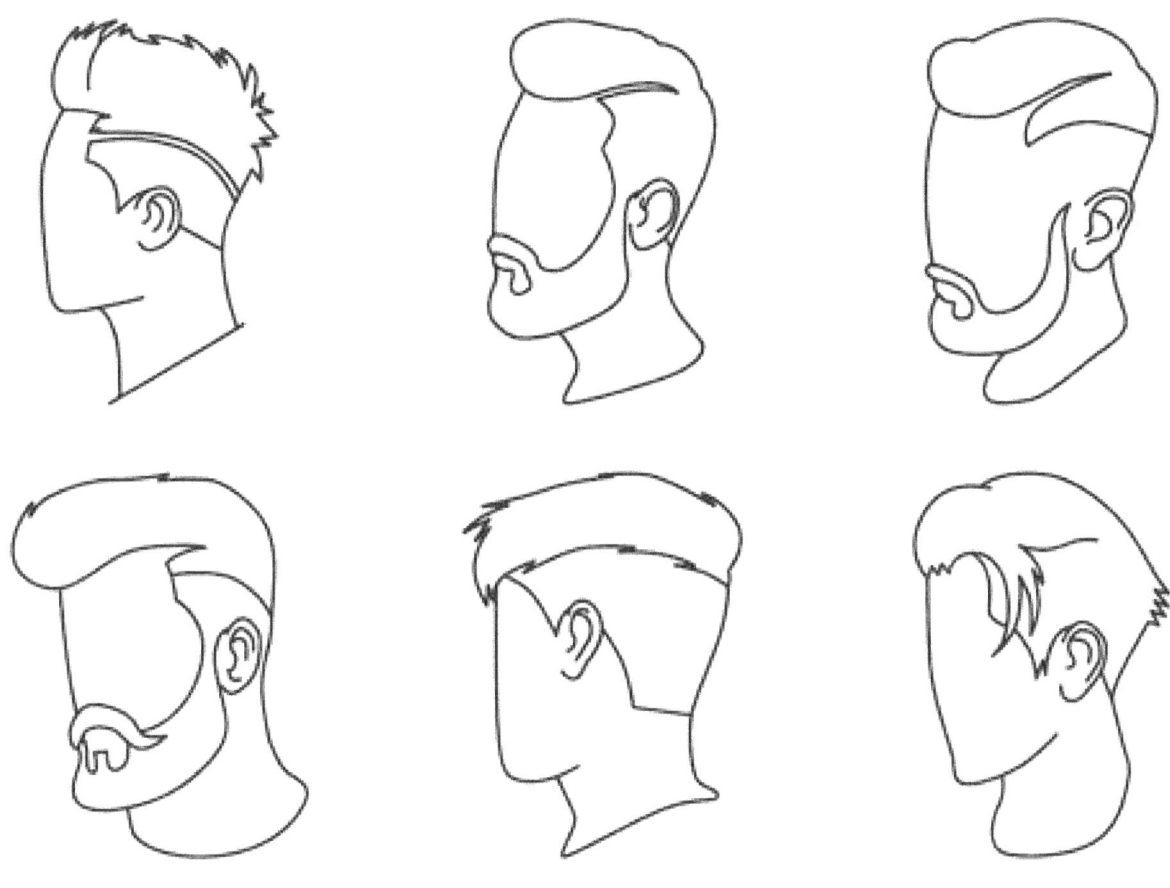

DRAW/SKETCH

WOMEN HEAD

DRAW/SKETCH

WOMEN HEAD

DRAW/SKETCH

BIG GIRL HEAD

DRAW/SKETCH

YOUNG MAN HEAD

DRAW/SKETCH

OLDER WOMAN HEAD

DRAW/SKETCH

OLD MAN HEAD

DRAW/SKETCH

OLDER MAN HEAD

DRAW/SKETCH

ASIAN BOY HEAD

DRAW/SKETCH

STYLISH WOMAN HEAD

DRAW/SKETCH

STYLISH WOMAN HEAD

DRAW/SKETCH

STYLISH WOMAN HEAD

DRAW/SKETCH

STYLISH WOMAN HEAD

DRAW/SKETCH

COOL WOMAN HEAD

DRAW/SKETCH

STYLISH MAN HEAD

DRAW/SKETCH

YOUNG BOY HEAD

DRAW/SKETCH

ONE TONE MAN HEAD

DRAW/SKETCH

ONE TONE MAN HEAD

DRAW/SKETCH

ONE TONE WOMAN HEAD

DRAW/SKETCH

PLAIN MAN HEAD

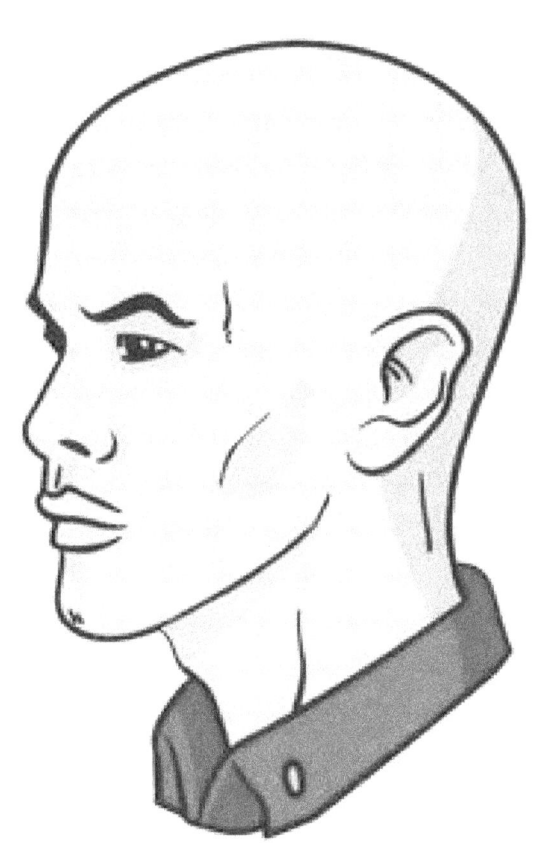

DRAW/SKETCH

TWO BOY HEADS

DRAW/SKETCH

YOUNG BOY HEAD

DRAW/SKETCH

YOUNG GIRL HEAD

DRAW/SKETCH

YOUNG GIRL HEAD

DRAW/SKETCH

FANCY WOMAN HEAD

DRAW/SKETCH

SIDE VIEW BOY HEAD

DRAW/SKETCH

SIDE VIEW GIRL HEAD

DRAW/SKETCH

SLEEPY GIRL HEAD

DRAW/SKETCH

CAMPER GIRL HEAD

DRAW/SKETCH

HAPPY BOY HEAD

DRAW/SKETCH

CURLY BOY HEAD

DRAW/SKETCH

CURLY HAIR GIRL HEAD

DRAW/SKETCH

CLIP, MOUTH AND
LETTER THINGS

FANCY FEMALE LIPS

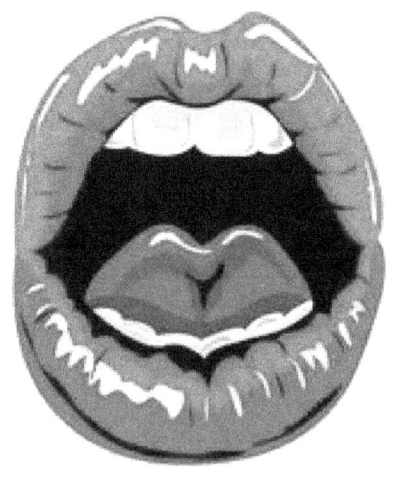
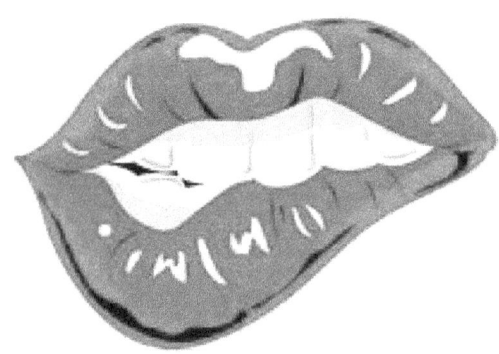

DRAW/SKETCH

FUN CARTOON TEETH

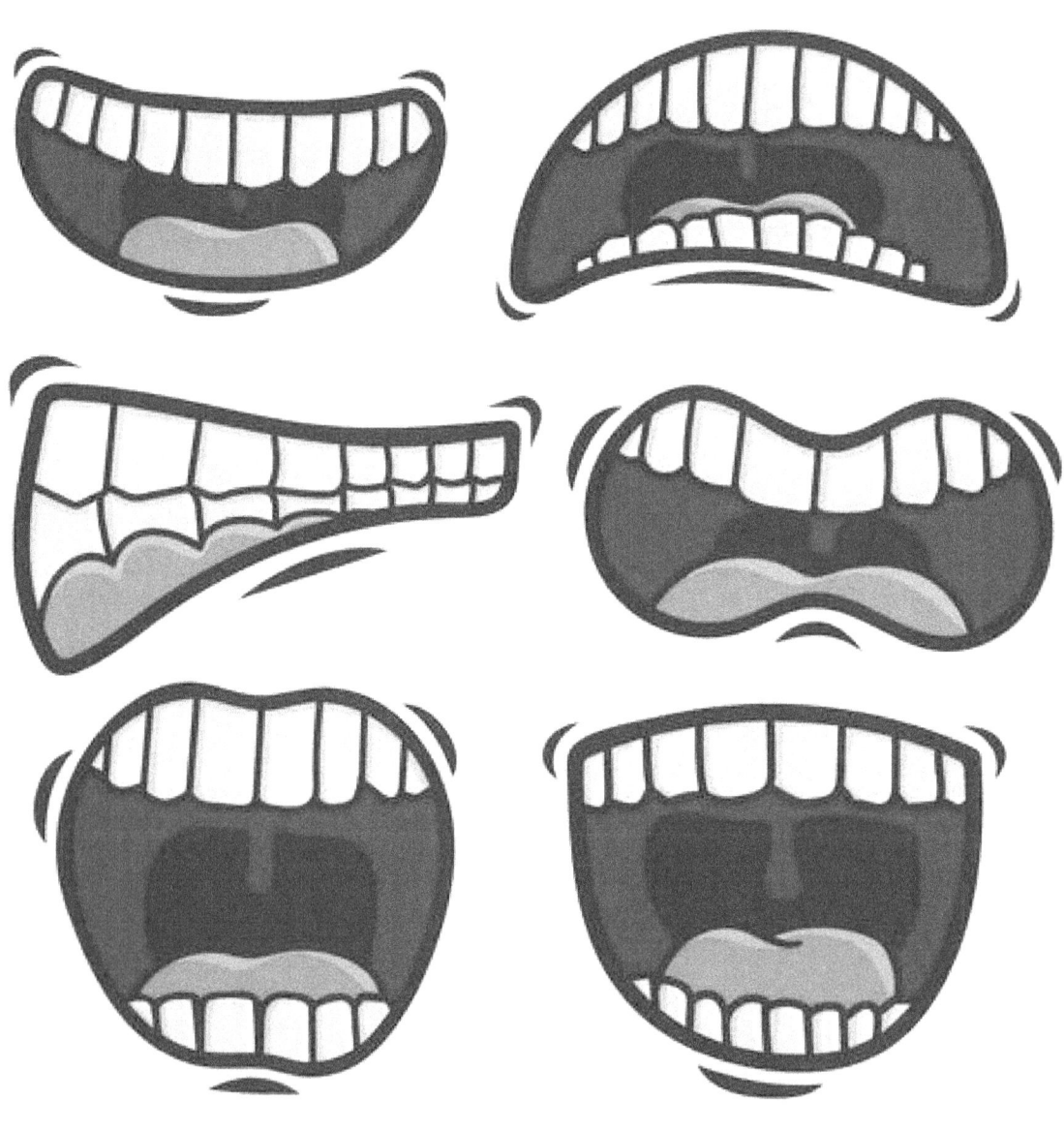

DRAW/SKETCH

FUN CARTOON LIPS

DRAW/SKETCH

One Tone Lip Drawings

DRAW/SKETCH

Two Tone Lip Drawings

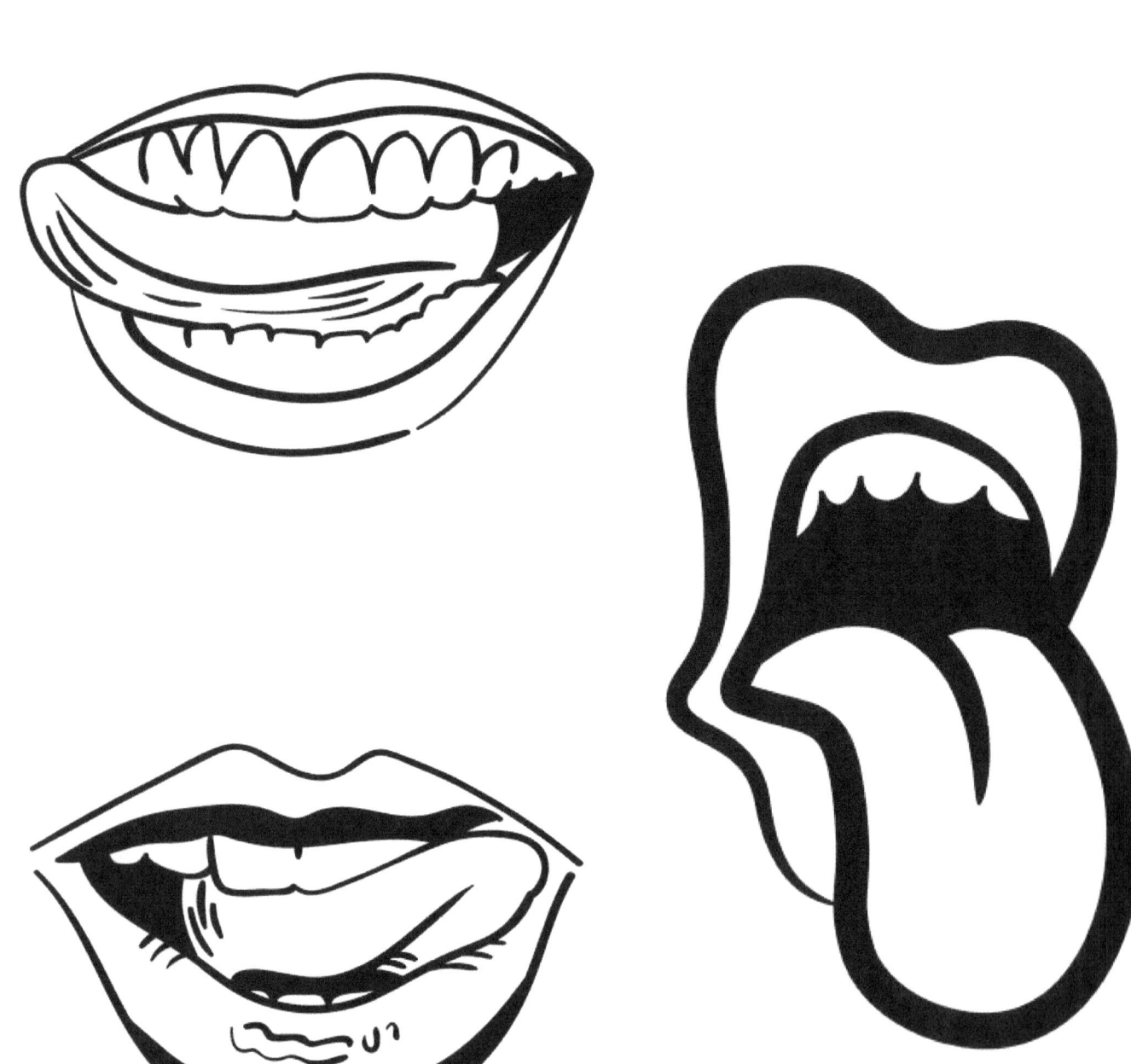

DRAW/SKETCH

FANCY LIPS AND TEETH

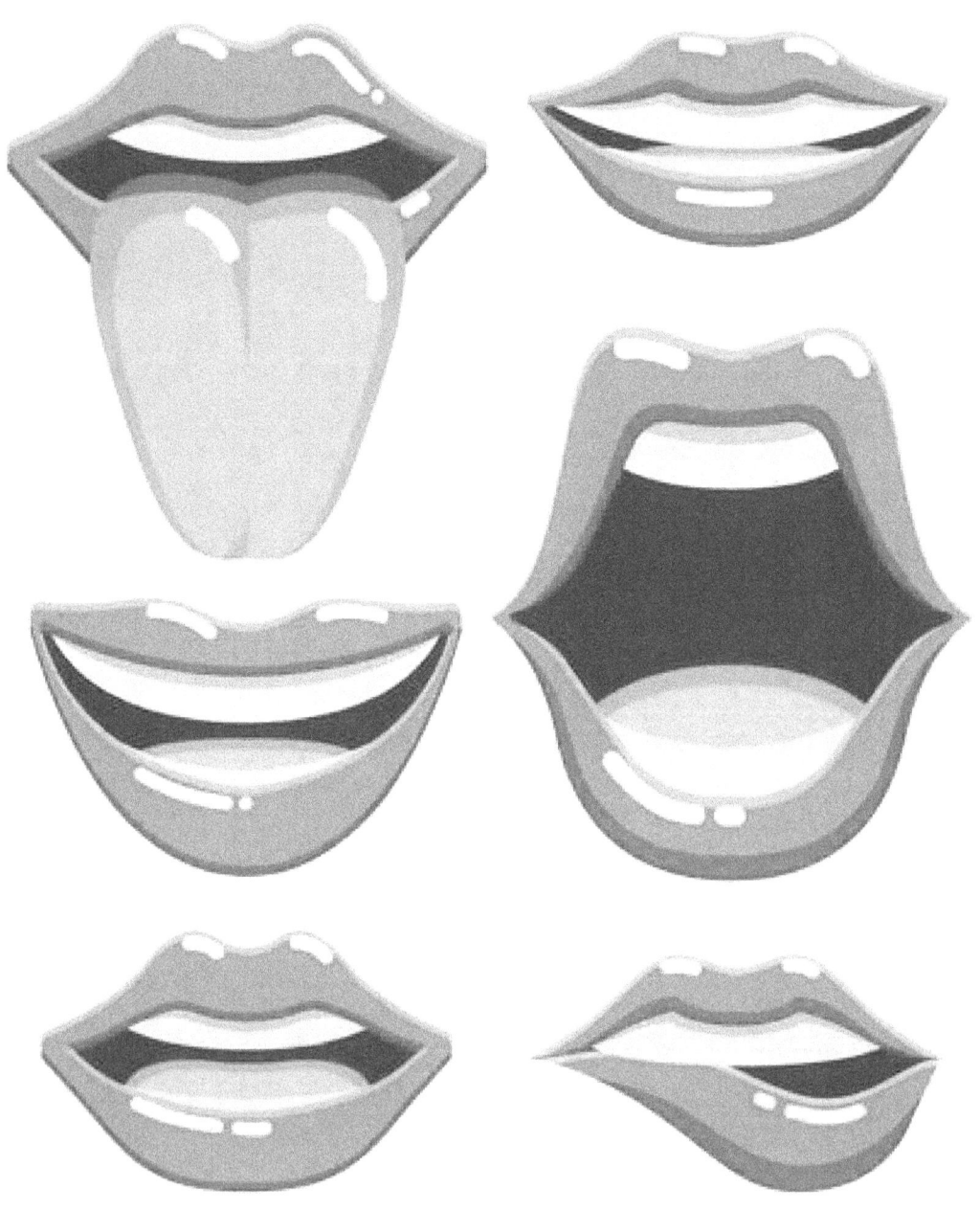

DRAW/SKETCH

MONSTER TEETH

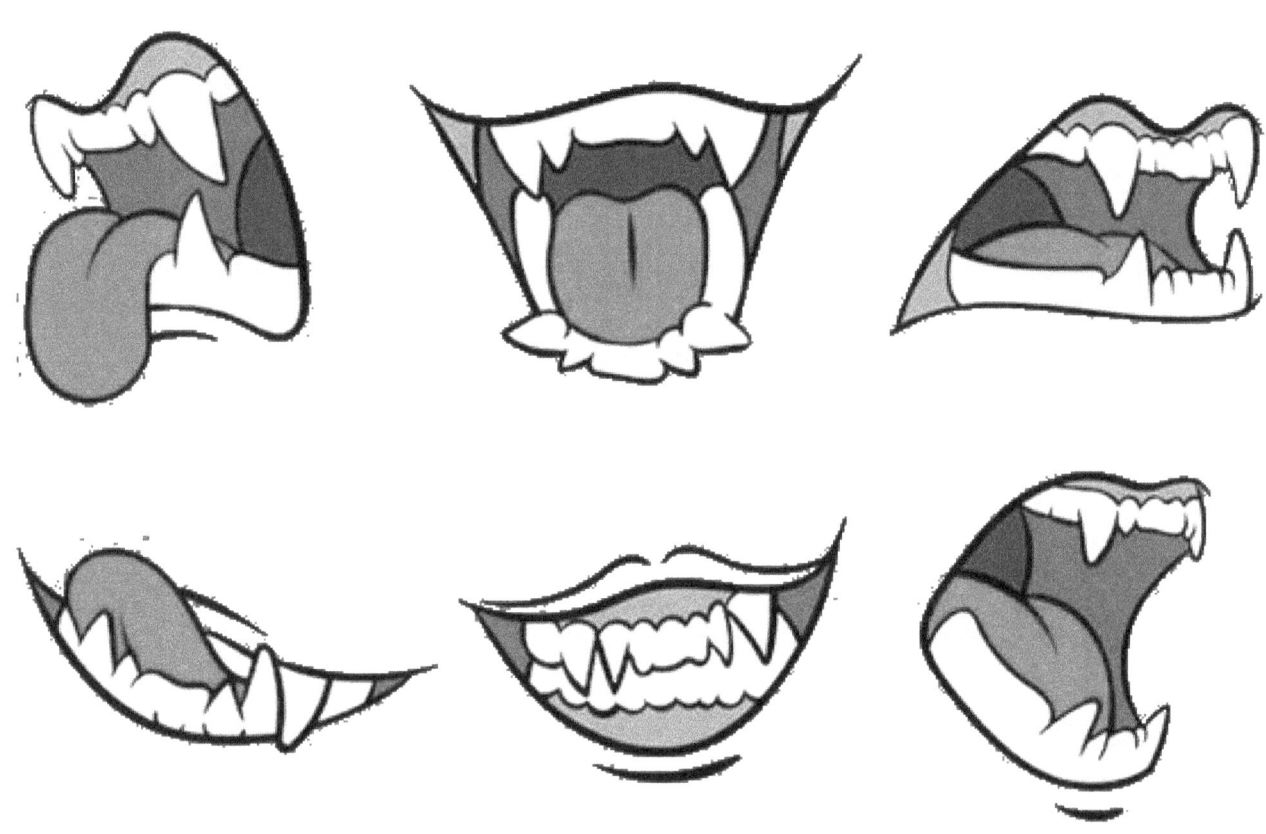

DRAW/SKETCH

CARTOON MOUTH

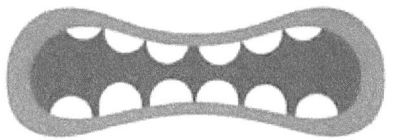
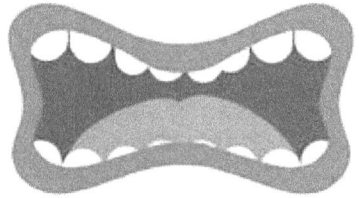

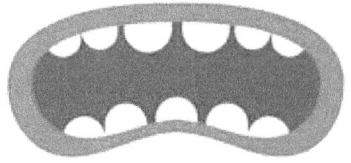

DRAW/SKETCH

BABY TEETH AND MOUTH

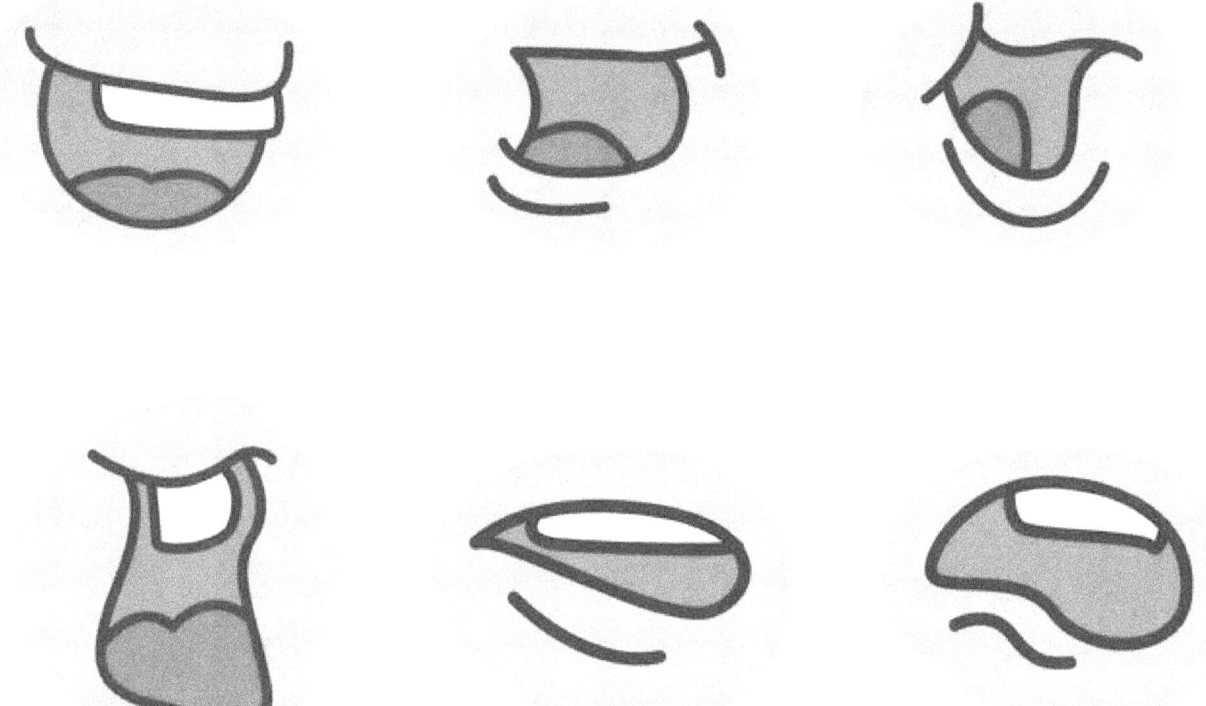

DRAW/SKETCH

EASY DRAWINGS

CARTOON ODD EYES

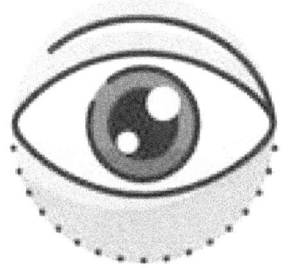
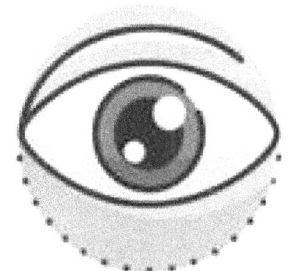
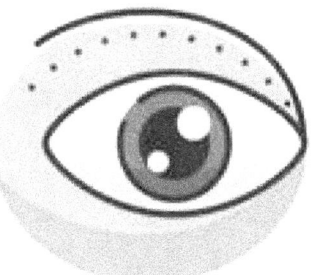
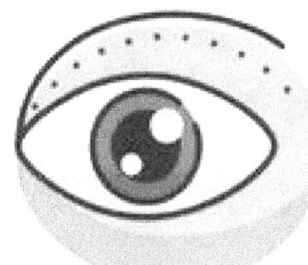

DRAW/SKETCH

BIG CARTOON EYES

DRAW/SKETCH

OPEN EYE DRAWINGS

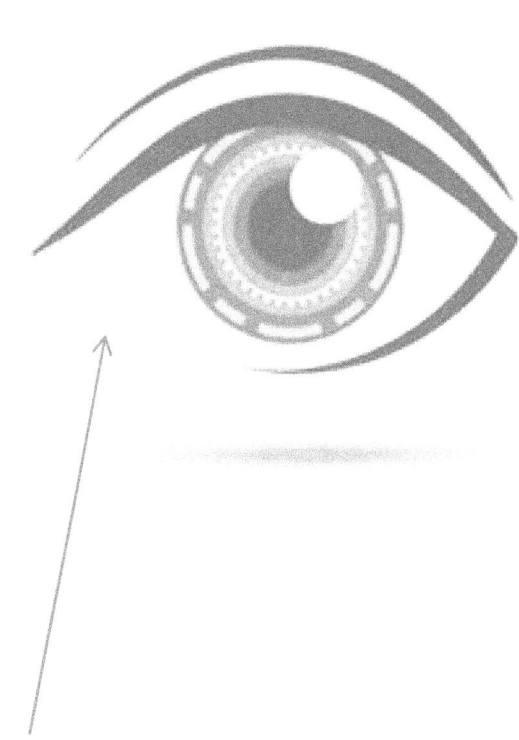

DRAW/SKETCH

CLOSED EYE DRAWINGS

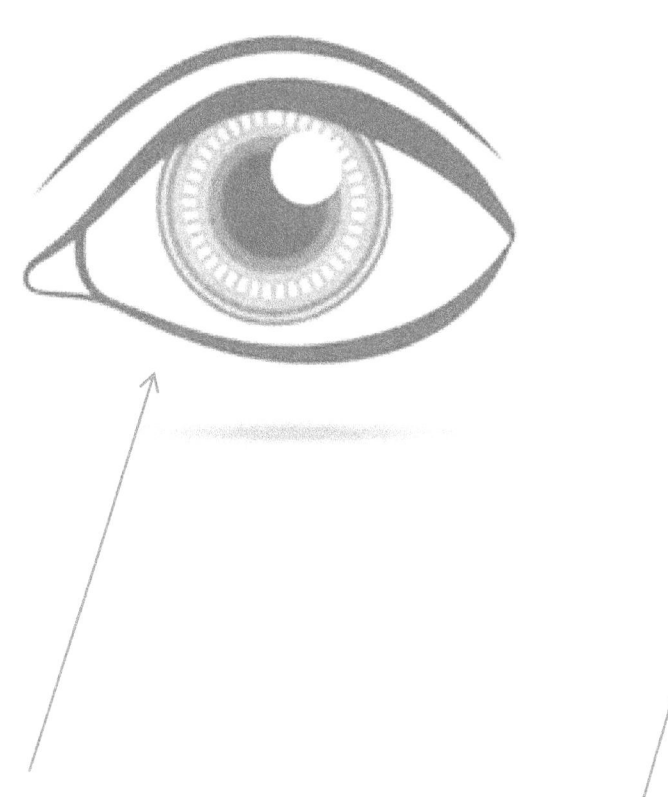
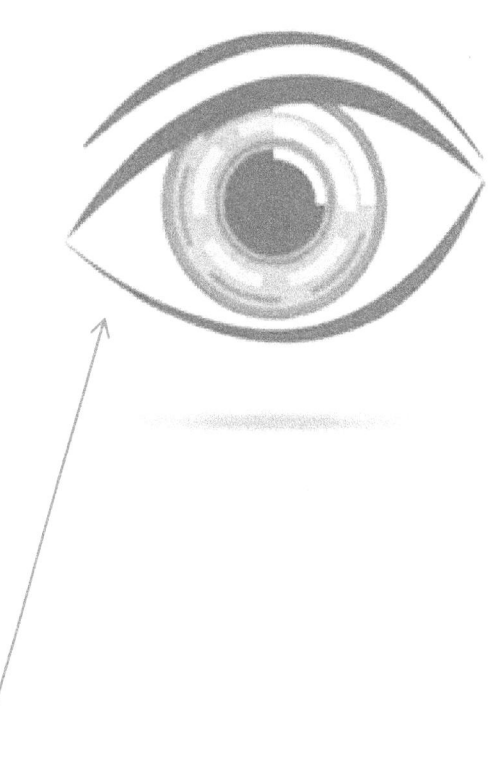

DRAW/SKETCH

ILLISTRATED EYE

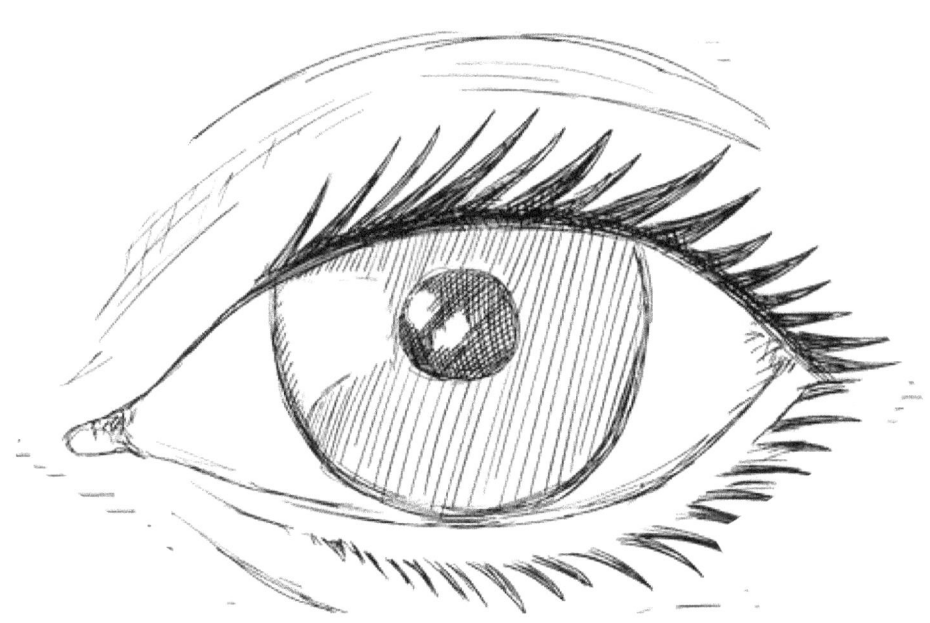

DRAW/SKETCH

DRAW/SKETCH

EXCITEMENT EYES

DRAW/SKETCH

SCARY EYES

DRAW/SKETCH

REALISTIC EYE

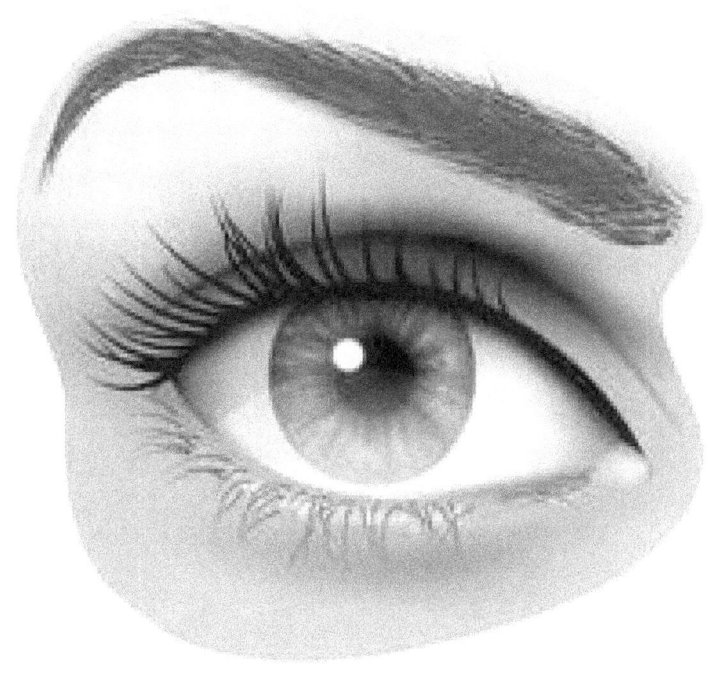

DRAW/SKETCH

ALIEN EYES

DRAW/SKETCH

REALISTIC NOSE

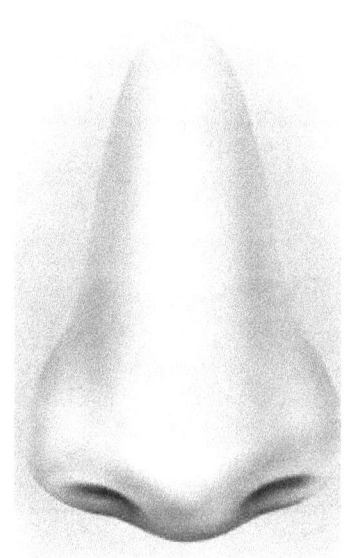

DRAW/SKETCH

SIDE NOSE VIEW

DRAW/SKETCH

TWO NOSE DIAGRAM

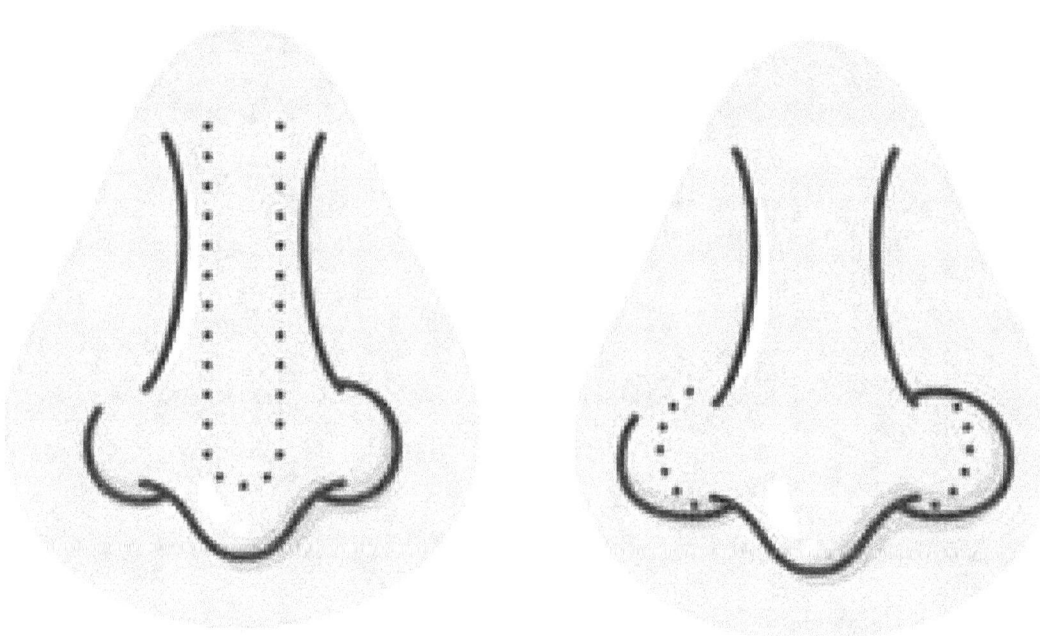

PENCIL NOSE

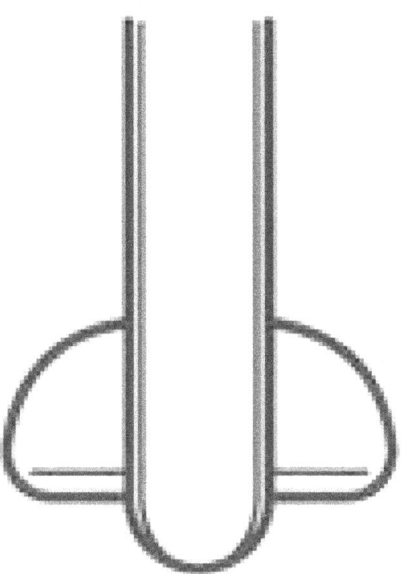

DRAW/SKETCH

PENCIL SIDE NOSE

DRAW/SKETCH

FRONT NOSE VIEW

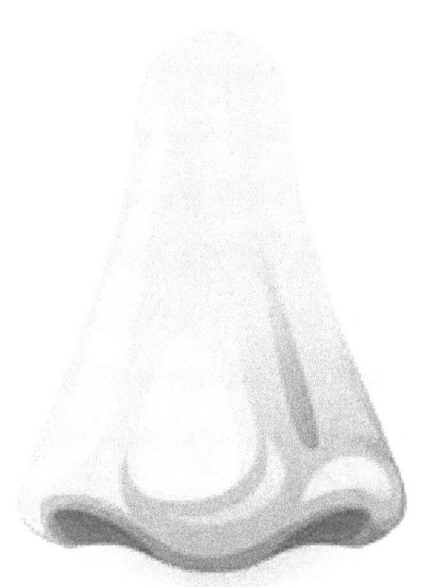

DRAW/SKETCH

REALISTIC EAR DRAWING

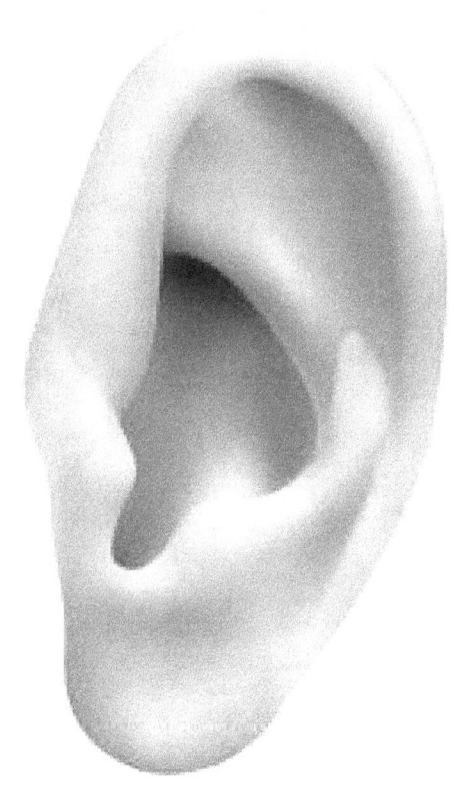

DRAW/SKETCH

EAR WITH TITLES

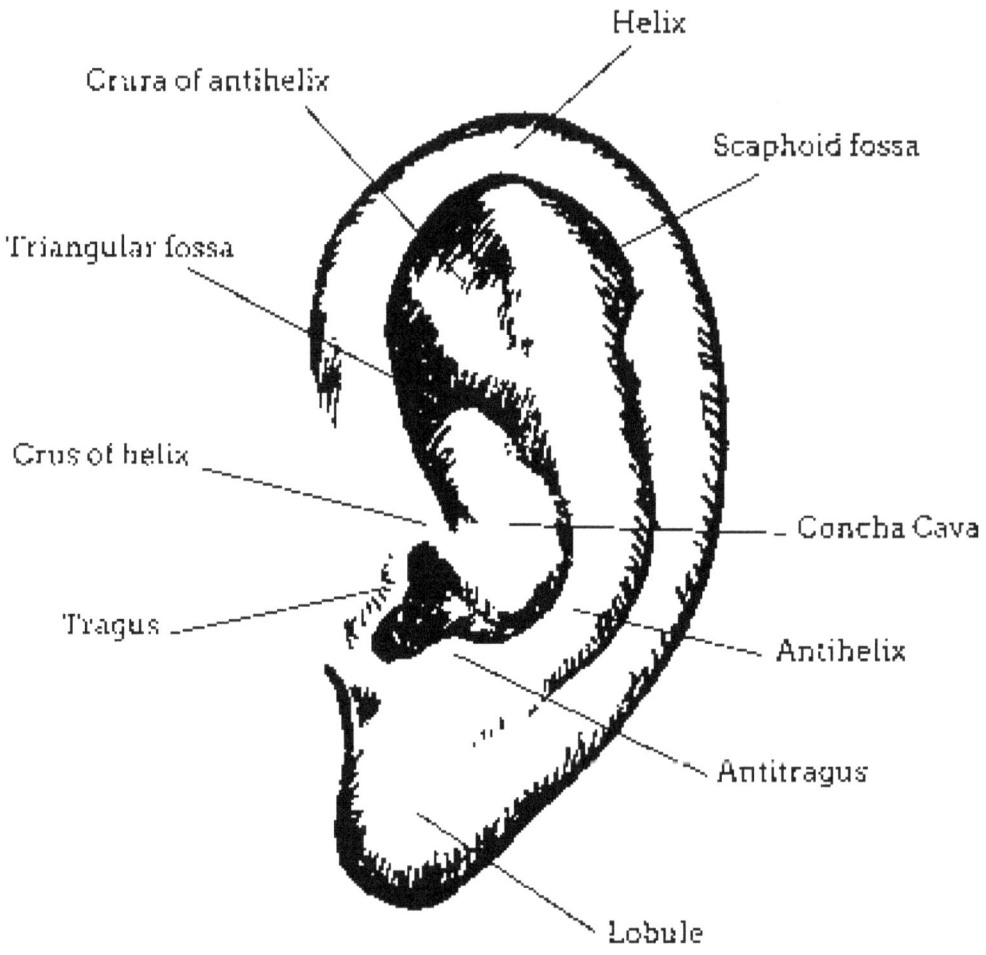

DRAW/SKETCH

CARTOON PENCIL EAR

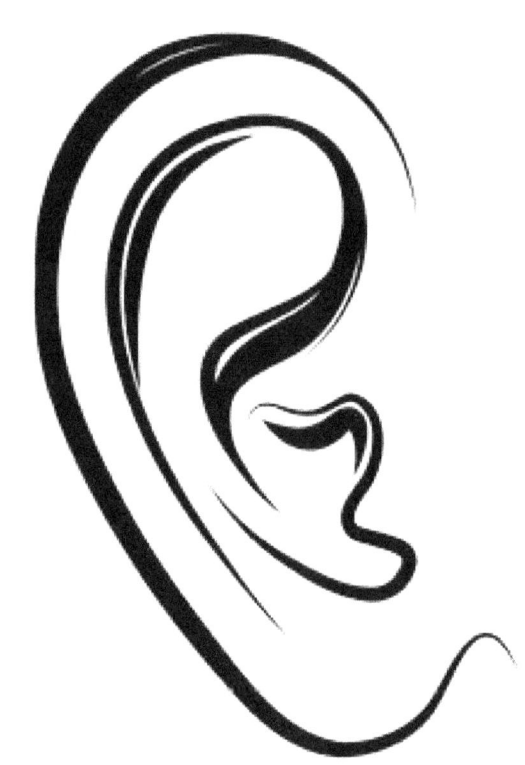

DRAW/SKETCH

CHIN DRAWINGS

CHIN DIAGRAM

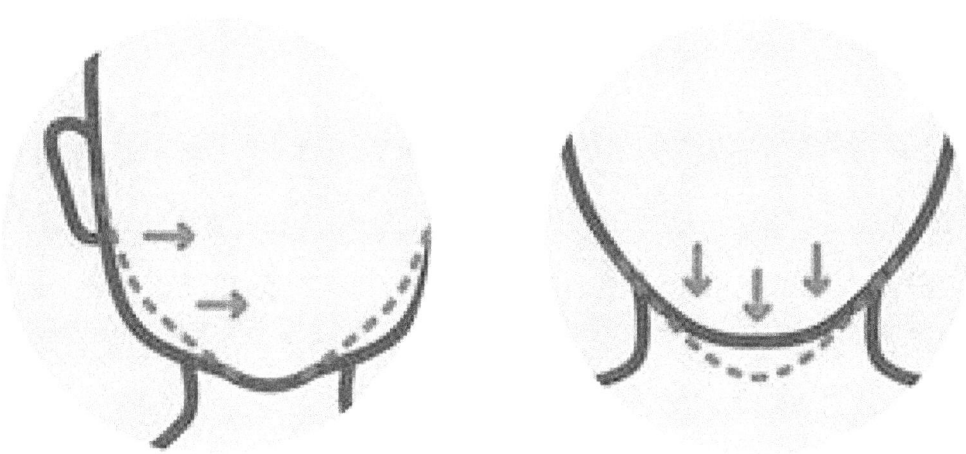

DRAW/SKETCH

CHIN DIAGRAM 2

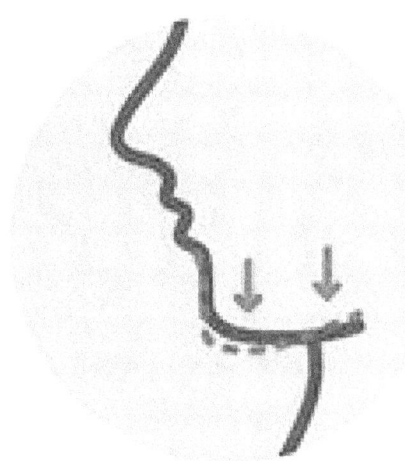 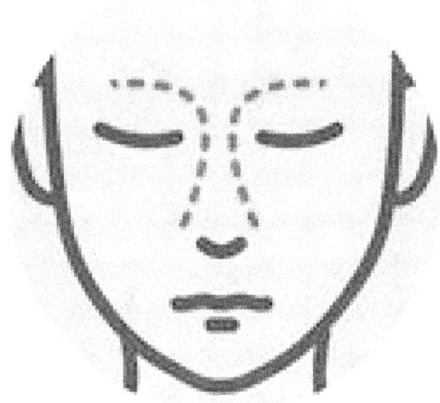

DRAW/SKETCH

CHIN WITH LINES

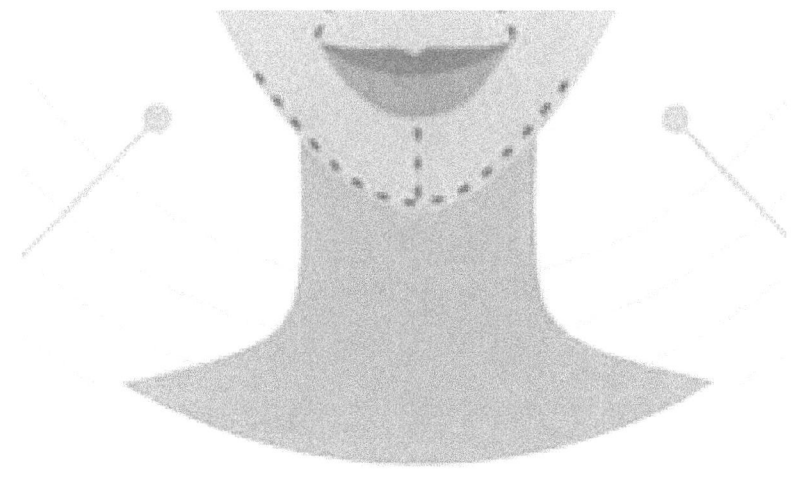

DRAW/SKETCH

CARTOON CHIN

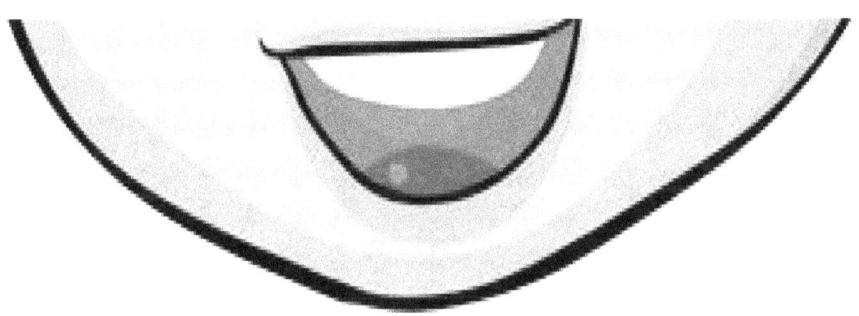

DRAW/SKETCH

DRAW/SKETCH

HAIR AND BEARD

DRAW/SKETCH

VARIOUS HAIR AND BEARDS

DRAW/SKETCH

FEMALE SIDE HAIR

DRAW/SKETCH

MALE FRONT HAIR VIEW

DRAW/SKETCH

BEARD ONLY DRAWING

DRAW/SKETCH

www.ingramcontent.com/pod-product-compliance
Lightning Source LLC
Chambersburg PA
CBHW081722100526
44591CB00016B/2463